THE FAST GOD CHOSE

SNATCH YOUR ~~WAIST~~ *soul*

> Including
> The 13-Day
> Customizable
> Water Fast
> That Changed
> My Life

An Empirical Guide to Fasting for Spiritual Freedom and Actualization

QUEEN MALIKA EWART

THE FAST GOD CHOSE

Disclaimer: I am not a medical professional, and this is not a medicinal book or guidance. I have zero scientific or medical evidence to support the assertions in this book. These assertions are empirically based on personal, firsthand experiences.

"[Rather] is this not the fast which I choose, To undo the bonds of wickedness, To tear to pieces the ropes of the yoke, To let the oppressed go free And break apart every [enslaving] yoke?"

ISAIAH 58:6 AMP

PREFACE

————— ৶৯৶৫ —————

Fasting is an endeavor that should not be taken lightly from a spiritual or physical standpoint. This imperative declaration is the crux of this book. I myself have embarked on fasts, of various sorts, that have led to both my spiritual and physical harm and devastation inconsistent motives and dangerous methods.

With that being said, there are two main warnings I want to give to anyone seeking to fast:

1. Always seek God through His word and prayer for divine affirmation of the appropriateness of the fast and

2. Seek the advice of a medical professional to evaluate their physical fitness for the purpose of fasting, specifically from all food except water, which is the main type of fasting utilized and explored in this text.

TABLE OF CONTENTS

FOREWORD

———— ꒰꒷꒦ ————

I wrote this book for the Believer who desired to fast for results–tangible, verifiable results. These results can only be obtained by fasting, as the Word of God calls us to fast. (Matthew 17:19- 21) AMP

"Then the disciples came to Jesus privately and asked, "Why could we not drive it out?" He answered, "Because of your little faith [your lack of trust and confidence in the power of God]; for I assure you and most solemnly say to you, if you have [living] faith the size of a mustard seed, you will say to this mountain, 'Move from here to there,' and [if it is God's will] it will move; and nothing will be impossible for you. 21 But this kind of demon does not go out except by prayer and fasting..."

There is a plethora of books, both medicinal and "spiritual," that have scientific citations and education on fasting as a dietary and loosely spiritual practice.

These books and other sources cite fasting as responsible for weight loss, physical healing, and overall wellness practices. I have experienced all of the above as a result of biblical fasting and by submitting related requests to God for healing and physical wellness during the fast. However, this guidance, this book, covers fasting as a weapon of spiritual warfare, a catalyst to spiritual growth, and a method of connecting to God for revelation–not fasting for weight loss, albeit a usual byproduct. We are not seeking to snatch our waists but to 'snatch our souls,' get our spiritual houses in order by cleansing, discarding the unnecessaries and making room for God to fill all the more.

The guidance provided is based on thorough biblical research on fasting using the Holy Bible as a main source and from my own personal experiences with fasting from 3 days to 30 days, consuming only water and the Word of God.

Ultimately, you must do what God leads you to do, and if you cannot hear or discern the voice of God or the unction of the Holy Spirit, or if you have interpreted what I just wrote about God's voice as solely hearing an audible and literal version of God's voice in your ear, please seriously reevaluate your spiritual readiness to embark on the fasting covered in this book....the Fast He has chosen. Isaiah 58:6

FOREWARNING

———————— ༈ ————————

You must, must, must come into this process at least wanting to submit to the will of God for your life. You do not have to completely understand what that means at this moment, but you must have the willingness to fully understand, and as your understanding increases, the willingness to adhere, submit, and obey. I cannot stress this enough. Starting this process by stepping on a literal or proverbial scale and checking for results daily is not the spirit in which a fast should be undertaken. This fast, among other requirements, must be an act of obedience to God's word. If you are reading this and saying, "Well, I am not a Christian," if you interpret that to mean you have not accepted Jesus Christ as your Lord and Savior and are not committed to a life of sanctification through the Word of God (the Holy Bible) and the Holy Spirit (all of which is the nature of being a Believer/Christian), then this book at this point is not for you. Although we will explore the subjects of confession, salvation, and sanctification, the endeavor this type of fast, is not for a non-Christian, neither should this type of fast be a first act of a new believer.

The beauty of our Lord is his arms are always open, you can become a Believer right now! Wherever and whomever you may be! I would implore a person who is inquiring into the nature of life as a Believer but does not yet identify as a Believer to first read these books and verses in the Bible in their entirety: the Gospel of John, Galatians Chapter 5, Romans

Chapter 9, Ephesians Chapter 5, and 2 Corinthians Chapter 13 (NO these are not prerequisites to being a Believer, but strong recommendations to understand who Christ is and what it means to be a Believer). If you choose to accept Christ as Lord of your life, CONGRATULATIONS AND WELCOME TO THE FAMILY!

As a new believer, before you fast, seek God through some of the scriptural resources in Chapter 1 of this book, prayer, your pastor, and/or other mature believers to determine if fasting, and thus this guide is right for you in this season of your life.

If you are a Believer and the reading suggested above for the non-believer seemed too cumbersome, then I would confidently assert that you are not a good candidate for the process and undertaking of the type of fast covered in *this* guidance.

There will be a lot, and I mean a lot, of reading as a part of this fasting process, and I recommend not using Google in this guide because the abusive or addictive use of technology is what many of us need to fast from in addition to food and in many cases permanently abstain from.

Repeatedly referring to technology as a main source of information during the fast will only erroneously reaffirm its essential nature in your life.

Furthermore, fasting should not be done with ungodly motives and certainly not by pregnant or breastfeeding women. If you are on a fast and you experience a medical emergency, cease fasting immediately. This did happen to me once, and it was because I was fasting to lose weight during breastfeeding and not with God in mind at all. My blood sugar dropped to coma- inducing levels, and I absolutely knew I was not okay. I was so pressured by this world's images and my own unhealthy self-image to 'snap back' after having a baby that it almost cost me my life.

Additionally, spontaneous eating during a fast "because you got hungry," drinking alcohol, or even having high levels of stress can be very dangerous during water fasting.

REMEMBER

The word "breakthrough" leads with "break." Breaking through will require multiple forms of breaking. Breaking habits, breaking mindsets, breaking chains of bondage, but most importantly, a broken and contrite spirit before God.

With Love, Good Stewardship, & Compassion,

'Queen' Malika Ewart

(my name Malika translates from Arabic to English as Queen)

INTRODUCTION

"But this kind does not go out but by prayer and fasting"

MATTHEW 17:21

Yes, some forms of stubbornness, bondage, lack of understanding, stagnation, lack of direction, and voids of revelation can only be eradicated by prayer and fasting. Fasting is no superpower or magic wand only accessible by the elite Christian; fasting can be successfully performed by any Believer *willing to fully submit and be broken before God*–the opposite of elitism.

I, like many believers, had heard this scripture quoted many times and, on numerous occasions, heard fasting referenced by Believers as a "hard-core Christian" undertaking. You know, for those deep Christians that know the deep stuff about God and pray long and stuff.

I grew up predominantly in the 'Baptist church,' literally from the cradle, and saw all forms of religiosity, most of which I either abhorred, assimilated, or thought were way too deep for me to ever understand. I used to think when people would shout or "catch the Holy Ghost," "boy, they was deep! Dem was the real Christians!" I often longed to be that deep and wondered what the day I got the Holy Ghost would look like, but I dare not fake it, whether out of fear of the Lord or sheer embarrassment; the jury is still out.

As a child, I never witnessed fasting firsthand in my home or family, albeit being the daughter of a preacher's kid and having a very religious, church-going family, but again, I knew it was deep, so I didn't judge mama or the fam, I just thought, "They ain't reached those levels yet."

My first experience with fasting was at 19 years old, at the first church I attended 'on my own.' I say on my own because I had decided to know God for myself and in that season, that required not attending church where my family was attending. This was a church one of my more estranged aunts attended, about 70 miles west of my then-home. I was not totally independent, but it was distant enough for me to explore God in a church setting in my own way, without familial emulation pressures, and since my aunt was there, it was safe enough that "if these folks were crazy," yeah.

The leaders of this church blended a lot of Africanism with Christianity (which I did not know at the time), so the teaching introduced me to concepts like chakras, kundalini, shekinah glory, crystals, and wheatgrass–you know, that deep stuff. In addition, albeit attending church all my life, I accepted Christ for myself at this church.

I was naive but ON FIRE and ready to go the distance to prove my heart's dedication and love for Christ outside of just being a "seat filler." This church was also very charismatic, so it was here that I could bellow, scream, shout, and dance freely; here is where I actually felt I could authentically worship past the "let the church stand, say amens, and hallelujahs that were provoked in my prior Baptist settings.

My newness as an independent believer combined with my newly found education in all of this new age seemingly deep Christian esoteric made me feel deep enough to volunteer when they asked if anyone out of our 16-person congregation would volunteer to fast for a little girl who, at the time, was four years old and going blind in one eye. I jumped out of my seat and eagerly volunteered, not really knowing what it meant besides that I would not eat. So that is what I did.

After the group prayer with all the volunteers, the pastor never followed up with me on the number of days or what to do, so I just said, okay, I guess I just don't eat until they make an announcement at church or send an email or something. Common sense told me to drink tons of water, and that is what I did.

Now, at this church, folks were always fasting, or rather, the leadership was always declaring fast, and in my carnal mind, I used to think, "These are some of the fattest, most fasting folks I've ever seen." Well, during this fast, something occurred that made it all make sense.

I was a part of the praise dance ministry at this church, and we rehearsed 2-3 times a week, so as a then-155-lb., 5'6, I was dancing and exercising very rigorously, running on just water for this entire fast. On about day 7, I arrived at Bible study, and still no announcement had been made as to when we were ending the fast or any other guidance. It was almost as if they had forgotten that folks volunteered. So, I leaned over to my husband and asked, "Hey, babe, do you think I should ask about the fast?" I was apprehensive because I remember in the group prayer, they admonished us not to tell people we were fasting (I now know the context and correct understanding of this), so I did not want it to seem as if I was complaining about the length. Just as I sat back straight at the table where we did Bible study, the pastor walked in with a lit birthday cake. Everyone started to sing happy birthday to the pastor's little son, who was about five at the time, and they then proceeded to cut the cake. They distributed pieces to the kids, myself, the pastors, and others that I was sure joined the same fast I was on?! I was so perplexed and could not help but ask the pastor, "Um, sis, is the fast over?" She retorted, "The fast?" I said, "Yes, the fast for --- that I and a few others agreed to last week for healing in her eye," and she said, "Oh, oh yes, so I prayed to God because it was (we will use Jessie as a fictitious name) Jessie's birthday, and He said we could break for cake and then go back." Now, I was a new believer, but I knew I had never read "Thou shalt break fast for Jessie's birthday." I went home so confused and disheartened. I had been going for seven days on just water, biting pieces of chicken, chewing it, and spitting it out, chewing on endless gum, and we could just stop for Jessie's birthday?!

Although I was discouraged by this, my heart for this little girl (who did end up healed, by the way) coupled with the snatchedness of my waistline encouraged me to continue for two more days, for a total of 9 days of water fasting on my first fast. Nine days of pure intentions, no guidance, random swallowing of a spoonful of macaroni here and a French fry there, Jessie's birthday (which became how we nick-named backsliding in our house for a season), angry outbursts, strife, and contention, and the start of an unhealthy dieting habit and pursuit of vanity.

This was my introduction to fasting. The fast that God did NOT choose.

INTRODUCTION SUMMARY

I cannot reiterate enough that this is not a diet. This is not a test of your willpower. This is not a race to super-Christian status, and this is not something you should do without fully understanding the nature of the undertaking. Especially if done biblically, THIS WILL NOT BE AN EASY OR QUICK PROCESS, NOTHING LIFE- CHANGING IS!

Not only will it not be easy or quick, but it will also require your 100% submission to God and His process. In this book I will give an example of what that looked like for me, but it will most certainly vary to varying degrees for you. No amount of intellect, psychologizing, philosophizing, theorizing, willpower, strength, aptitude, or credibility will get you through it, period. Going into this, relying on those things will ensure, with an infallible assuredness that you will fail!

You cannot say I did not tell you so. You can be the prayer and fasting warrior of the century, and if this process is not done relying solely and only on the power and might of God our Father and the partnering of the Holy Spirit, all by the grace of Jesus Christ, you will not succeed or see results.

ISAIAH 58:1- 14
AMPLIFIED STUDY BIBLE ZONDERVAN

OBSERVANCES OF FASTS

[1]"Cry aloud, do not hold back; Lift up your voice like a trumpet, And declare to My people their transgression And to the house of Jacob their sins. [2] "Yet they seek Me day by day and delight [superficially] to know My ways, As [if they were in reality] a nation that has done righteousness And has not abandoned (turned away from) the ordinance of their God. They ask of Me righteous judgments; They delight in the nearness of God. [3] 'Why have we fasted,' they say, 'and You do not see it? Why have we humbled ourselves and You do not notice?' Hear this [O Israel], on the day of your fast [when you should be grieving for your sins] you find something you desire [to do], And you force your hired servants to work [instead of stopping all work, as the law teaches]. [4] "The facts are that you fast only for strife and brawling and to strike with the fist of wickedness. You do not fast as you do today to make your voice heard on high. [5] "Is a fast such as this what I have chosen, a day for a man to humble himself [with sorrow in his soul]? Is it only to bow down his head like a reed And to make sackcloth and ashes as a bed [pretending to have a repentant heart]? Do you call this a fast and a day pleasing to the Lord? [6] "[Rather] is this not the fast which I choose, To undo the bonds of wickedness, To tear to pieces the ropes of the yoke, To let the oppressed go free And break apart every [enslaving] yoke? [7] "Is it not to divide your bread with the hungry And bring the homeless poor into the house; When you see the naked, that you cover him, And not to hide yourself from [the needs of] your own flesh and blood? [8] "Then your light will break out like the dawn, And your healing (restoration, new life) will quickly spring forth; Your righteousness will go before you [leading you to peace and prosperity], The glory of the Lord will be your rear

guard. [9] "Then you will call, and the Lord will answer; You will cry for help, and He will say, ' Here I am.' If you take away from your midst the yoke [of oppression], The finger pointed in scorn [toward the oppressed or the godly], and [every form of] wicked (sinful, unjust) speech, [10] And if you offer yourself to [assist] the hungry And satisfy the [a]need of the afflicted, Then your light will rise in darkness And your gloom will become like midday.[11] "And the Lord will continually guide you, And satisfy your soul in scorched and dry places, And give strength to your bones; And you will be like a watered garden, And like a spring of water whose waters do not fail. [12] "And your people will rebuild the ancient ruins; You will raise up and restore the age-old foundations [of buildings that have been laid waste]; You will be called Repairer of the Breach, Restorer of Streets [b]with Dwellings.[13] "If you turn back your foot from [[c]unnecessary travel on] the Sabbath, From doing your own pleasure on My holy day, And call the Sabbath a [spiritual] delight, and the holy day of the Lord honorable, And honor it, not going your own way Or [d]engaging in your own pleasure Or speaking your own [idle] words,[14] Then you will take pleasure in the Lord, And l will make you ride on the high places of the earth, And l will feed you with the [promised] heritage of Jacob your father; For the mouth of the Lord has spoken."

PACKING FOR THE JOURNEY

───────── ༓ ─────────

The type of fast expounded upon in this writing is a spiritual discipline prompted by the Holy Spirit in you, whether for the benefit of yourself or others.

Fasting is a journey–a very intimate journey between you and God. In my experience, sometimes God calls others to join in with you in fasting by either commanding you to ask specific people to fast with you, or by someone else asking to join your personal fast, or you being requested to participate in fasting called by someone else; either way, it is still a very intimate and personal journey. I have participated in both corporate church fasts and fasts called by others; those types of fasts are not the subject of this writing, but the intimate processes of prepping, trekking, and reflecting that are part of the journey of personal fasting can be applied to your participation in corporate and group fasts.

No journey is undertaken or should be undertaken without preparation; fasting is no exception. There is a physical preparation that should take place to prepare your body–God's temple–for fasting as well as spiritual preparation. There are times when the urgency to fast has just been dropped on me by the Holy Spirit, and I cannot physically prepare as much as would be ideal; however, fasting should never skip spiritual preparation.

The process of prepping may take anywhere from 24 hours to a week, depending on how engaged you are in work and life activities and what exactly God is calling you to do. During the prep time, you are not fasting; you are preparing for the fast and setting the spiritual and physical atmosphere for the journey.

I was led to make this guide as practical and simplistic as possible. In that spirit, **Part 1,** 'Packing for the Journey,' will be broken down into steps. So, open your spiritual luggage, and let's get to packing and prepping for the life- changing journey of going on the Fast that God chooses.

STEP 1

WRITING OUT YOUR REQUEST, OBJECTIVES, & INTENTIONS

———— ৵৻৶৻ ————

I n my first draft of this guide, I had Step 2, 'Understanding Fasting' as Step 1 because, of course, I am writing in hindsight about performing a biblical fast and know what looks most "Christian-like" but that was not the order I performed the tasks when embarking on my life-changing fast.

I have switched the order to reflect what I actually did because this guide is based on my actual journey and for the following other reasons:

Chiefly, if you complete Step 2 first and you are anything like me, you will psych yourself into writing objectives that you think God wants you to write and not what your soul is panting for, and what led you to this process in the first place.

You will keep masking, watering down, and religiousizing what is in your heart. God knows your heart, but He wants you to tell Him your heart from your heart. He also wants you to see a zoomed-out, birds-eye view of your heart. In order that you may fully conceptualize and understand the scripture that says, "For My thoughts are not your thoughts, Nor are your ways My ways," declares the Lord" (Isaiah 55).

In order to recognize this distance between our thoughts and God's, we have to really lay out our thoughts and our ways honestly. Now, I am not implying that our objectives done our way will inherently be wrong or even far from what God wants for us; however, as you will discover through this journey, God only answers honest requests. In the end, or maybe even some way through this journey, you will be so grateful you objectively laid out your request and intentions from a raw, honest, and candid view.

Lastly, the reason you need to write out your request, objectives, and intentions before studying first is to get them out already!

What do you want to see happen in this process? What answers are you seeking? This is what we all came for–to get what we need from this process, and it will just feel better to get it all out. It did for me.

My unfiltered concerns were chief and top of my fasting guide, and GOD ADDRESSED THEM ALL. This is my 100% truth; He answered all my requests favorably, all of them. But, oh, baby, the real gems were the things I did not intend to gain! The true fruits of the fast, which had very little to do with my objective pre-study request, made my request look like a drop in an ocean of water. Is there really anything too hard for God? (Jeremiah 32:27)

I am certainly not laying the foundation for you to perceive God as our genie and fasting as rubbing the genie lamp, and VIOLA! I am simply giving my honest testimony that every time I have conducted a biblically sound, spirit- led, and sustained fast, God answered every prayer and addressed every objective before the fast concluded. For the first time, within hours of my total submission to the process, one of my main fasting requests was answered.

ACTION

So, use the format provided in Appendix A, or use your own writing space or forum, and list out every single thing you want God to accomplish over the course of the fast.

STEP 2
GET A THOROUGH UNDERSTANDING OF FASTING

———— ೨ ೧೯ ೬ ————

Required: *Concordance, Bible dictionary, time*

Fasting- *Voluntarily depriving oneself for a divinely appointed time of food along with things of grave desire or the like.*

Successful fasting is fasting in obedience and satisfaction of our Lord and Savior. To be successful at fasting, you must understand what it is and what it is not. I know it seems intuitive, yet 90% of all the fasting I had done in my life as a Believer was without completing Step 2- 'Understanding Fasting!'

Like many things we do in our lives–cooking a dish for the first time, getting a haircut– or a new set of lashes. Step 1 will take the longest the first time you do it, and later you will be enhancing your understanding rather than building it. After this fast, even though you would've gained most of the resources to understand and complete a biblical fast, each time you pack for your fasting journey, you will revisit these tools and resources to make sure you understand them enough for the specific journey God uniquely planned for that particular fast.

HOW NOT TO FAST

As I stated, 90% of all the fasting I had done in my life as a Believer was done without even considering Step 2, which again is getting a thorough understanding of fasting. My process before I started to biblically fast looked like this:

1. Tell God what I need from God.

2. Starve

3. Tadaaah!! Where are my blessings, God?!

- Shame.

As I look back over those experiences, I feel so sorrowful for the worship I robbed God of and the miracles that I left unboxed due to my ignorance. "My people are destroyed for lack of knowledge [of My law, where I reveal My will]." (Hosea 4:6)

Due to my lack of knowledge and understanding about such a powerful spiritual weapon, my efforts usually ended up backfiring on me. I mean, it's like just going to a gun store, purchasing an automatic rifle, and thinking, "Okay, you just pull the trigger, right?" BACKFIRE! BACKFIRE! BACKFIRE! "And with all your acquiring, get understanding [actively seek spiritual discernment, mature comprehension, and logical interpretation]." (Proverbs 4:7)

Fasting can definitely be likened to a military assault rifle against the enemy and his strongholds when used biblically, but in the wrong hands with the wrong motives BACKFIRE, it can be deadly, literally, and spiritually.

Every time I fasted before seeking God's guidance on how to fast, I would be so irritated from hunger, weak, and frustrated. Y'all, I would have all-out cussing matches with my husband WHILE I WAS FASTING! And, of course, in my non-renewed mind and uninformed arrogance, I counted it all as "the devil attacking me because of my sacrifice"! Ha! Not, definitely not, the fast that God chose to set the captives free.

HOW TO PERFORM STEP 2 (8 ACTIONS)

So, let's get into this. Like a recipe, I pray that you let God work it for you as God did for me.

(STEP 2) ACTION 1: GO TO YOUR CONCORDANCE AND LOOK UP THE WORD FAST OR FASTING

Look up the word "fast" or "fasting" in your Bible dictionary and write out the definition. Thereafter, using your Bible's index and/or Concordance, write out every instance scripturally of the word being mentioned in the Bible and the corresponding context, if provided.

In my personal guide, I provided the scriptures that I compiled to guide my first study of fasting when I embarked on my first comprehensive, life-changing fast. However, this is not to be viewed as an exhaustive list.

I compiled this list by doing this same process through my Amplified Study Bible's concordance, and after praying, I chose the main spiritual focal points to guide my fast in duration and categorical focus.

Here are scriptures and concepts I extracted from my study that aided in the construction of my fasting outline and guide.

A. Fasting Generally: Isaiah 58, Matthew 4.

B. Occasions for fasting in the Bible

1. To prepare to receive God's law: EXODUS 34; DEUTERONOMY 9.

2. To prevent God's wrath: DT 9:18

3. To prepare for the day of Atonement: LEVITICUS 16

4. To show sorrow at time of death: 1 SAMUEL 31, 2 SAMUEL 1

5. To accompany confessions & showing of sorrow for sin: 1 KING 21, NEHEMIAH 9, JONAH 3, NUMBERS 14

6. As a part of repentance for sins: JONAH 3, JOEL 2. To show humility: PSALM 35, PSALM 135

7. To pray in time of national need: 2 CHRONICLES 2, EZRA 8, ESTHER 4, JOEL 2

8. To accompany deep personal prayer: 2 SAMUEL 12, NEHEMIAH 1, DANIEL 9. ACTS 9

9. To prepare for mission work or identify personal ministry: ACTS 13, ACTS 14. As an act of obedience- LEVITICUS 26

10. To gain courage: 2 Samuel 12

11. To gain clarity on decision-making/To learn the will of God: DANIEL 9

C. How Not to Fast

1. Setting out to do leisurely and self-serving things: ISAIAH 58:3, 13-14

2. Out of obligation: JEREMIAH 14:12

3. To be noticed: ISAIAH 58:3-7, JEREMIAH 14:12, ZECHARIAH 7:4310, MATTHEW 6:16-18, LUKE 18: 9-14

(STEP 2) ACTION 2: TAKE ABOUT 8 HRS (OVER 1-2 DAYS) TO STUDY THE SCRIPTURES YOU HAVE COMPILED ON FASTING

Studying for me is:

1. Praying before engaging with God's word for His revelation.

2. Reading the scriptures to myself and aloud.

3. Cross-referencing other scriptures when either directed by footnotes, a concordance, or the Holy Spirit.

4. Intentionally reflecting and "meditating" on what God is telling me through the scriptures by comparing and matching the themes and messages of the scriptures with my life in the past, present, and future.

5. Writing out the full scripture in my notebook/writing forum when it deeply resonates.

Repeat the above five steps for every scripture you identify that describes fasting and/or, if you are using my list, for every scripture listed above. Writing or typing out the full scriptures will be time-consuming and may seem cumbersome, but it is a necessary part of "meditating on the scripture." After all, fasting is a time to be entrenched in God and God's word.

Again, this process will take time.

TIPS, EXAMPLES & EXPERIENCES

During your study, extract what fasting is according to the scripture and what it is not. Identify why people fasted throughout the Bible and the context in which they did so. The goal is to get an overall understanding of the purposes of fasting throughout the Word of God.

In my experience, it took me two days, about 4- 5 hours per day, to conduct a thorough study of fasting as a spiritual and biblical undertaking. This was not a scholarly theological, theoretical, or exhaustive biblical study, and I am not suggesting that an exhaustive study of fasting can be completed in two days. This is the amount of time it took for me to understand fasting enough for my experience level to embark on it as a spiritual undertaking with confidence.

(STEP 2) ACTION 3: EXTRACT FOCAL POINTS FROM YOUR STUDY OF FASTING AS GUIDES FOR YOUR FAST

I used the scriptures I attained through my fast study, which is listed above, to extract points I needed to focus on either because the Bible instructed that it should be a component of the fast, i.e., repentance, or because God was leading me to commune with Him further in that area, i.e., Writing the Vision. I allocated one day of fasting and prayer to each focal; more on this below.

(STEP 2) ACTION 4: EVALUATE WHICH VIRTUES YOU NEED TO BUILD IN YOUR LIFE TO AID IN ACCOMPLISHING THE REQUEST YOU LISTED IN STEP 1 'WRITING OUT *YOUR* REQUEST, OBJECTIVES AND INTENTIONS'

As Pastor Voddie Baucham states, and I am paraphrasing,

Righteousness, or right living, can only be accomplished by understanding and accepting the indicatives and imperatives of God.

Indicatives: Who God says we are. Imperatives: What we are commanded to do.

The imperatives are only possible as humans because of the indicatives.

This is in line with my warning in the introduction that if you are not a Believer, meaning you have not been converted and accepted Christ as Lord of your life, you cannot embody any of the indicatives, and thus it will be impossible to obtain the virtues or "imperatives" that will be necessary to see the request you made in Step 1 actualize.

After you have identified the virtues, you need to build in your life, note them in the outline provided in addition to the request you made. The virtues you identify in this step will also become individual focal points for the fast.

(STEP 2) ACTION 5: OUTLINE THE STUDIES FOR EACH FOCAL POINT CHOSEN

After completing the four action steps outlined above, I ended up with 13 spiritual focal points, and thus I fasted for 13 days, giving myself one day to focus on each precept, request, or virtue. Had I ended up with 14 focal points, I would've gone 14 days; if I ended up with four focal points, four days, and so on and so forth. These days, I am sometimes led to allocate several days of fasting and prayer to one focal point and it is not always 1:1.

For each daily focal point you extracted, you will perform the same study process you did to understand Fasting as a concept: 1) Define through the Bible dictionary, 2) Expound the definition by getting scriptures from the concordance or index.

TIPS, EXAMPLES & EXPERIENCES

For example, one of my Objectives/Request I stated in Step 1 was "Breaking Spiritual Strongholds off of my Husband and Children," as I studied fasting in Actions 1& 2, God revealed to me that one of the virtues that would be required for that process was courage. I, therefore, made courage one focal point in the fast, found scriptures relating to courage, and took courage as a focal point through the Step 2 Action 1 process of identifying scripture. Write down the scriptures found as you will be further studying, praying, and meditating on them (Step 2, Action 1-2) during the fast. During the fast, you will become aware of other scriptures on the daily focal points you choose as you broaden your study to other tools, commentaries, multimedia aids, and sermons.

(STEP 2) ACTION 6: SEEK GOD AND DECIDE ON WHAT YOUR DAYS WILL LOOK LIKE

This step is critical. A large objective of fasting is to seek God, focus on God, and allow space for God to have your undivided attention, not to lose weight or observe rituals. If you do not properly structure your day to alleviate as much stress, obligation, and activity as you can, it will be physically and spiritually draining and ultimately counterproductive.

Ideally, I would recommend a sabbatical, meaning your fasting days are free from work and unnecessary activity. Personally, I did work during my fast, but from home, for a maximum of 2 hours per day. Most days, I did not work at all. I did exercise for the first few days of the fast but later lacked the interest, energy, or perceived prioritization of physical exercise.

I am married with two children, and I lead a mentorship ministry online during that time; I did not "take off" from those obligations. If you are married you must obtain spousal consent to fast from sex. (1 Corinthians 7:5-11)

Here are some things to consider when organizing your time during fasting:

1. TIMING OF DAY

I started my days before sunrise and 'kids-rise', usually 5:00 to 6:00 am. I chose to dedicate 8 - 12 hours to study, prayer, and worship. I took my cue from Nehemiah 9:1-3.

> [1] *"Now on the twenty-fourth day of this month, the Israelites assembled with fasting and in sackcloth and with dirt [a]on their heads.* [2] *The [b]descendants of Israel (Jacob) separated themselves from all foreigners, and stood and confessed their sins and the wrongdoings of their fathers.* [3] *While they stood in their places, they read from the Book of the Law of the Lord their God for a fourth of the day and for another fourth [of it] they confessed [their sins] and worshiped the Lord their God."*

Again, seek God for what He requires from you in your fasting process.

2. ENVIRONMENT

As a family woman, my family, albeit not participating in the not-eating portion of the fast, did sometimes participate in the study and worship time; I reserved most of the prayer times for intimate and private prayer with God and me.

On certain days, based on the focus of that day, I choose specific locations to complete my prayer and worship so as to be strategic about having a quiet time or a fitting setting.

Organize your day with these factors in mind to avoid feelings of overwhelm and stress that may lead to eating or, worse, to invoking spirits that are counterproductive to the growth catalyzed by fasting.

TIPS, EXAMPLES & EXPERIENCES

For example, on the day I chose the focal point to be the confession of sins, I started that day before sunrise at a local private beach and took my water, Bible, blanket, and music player. I poured out my heart to God in confession, and God was faithful to bring things to my mind that I didn't even realize I needed to confess. I then symbolically 'self-baptized' in that ocean. No one was around, but me and God, and this felt more real than both times I was baptized, once as a child and another as a young adult.

(STEP 2) ACTION 7: RESEARCH AND COMPILE MULTIMEDIA STUDY AND WORSHIP TOOLS TO SUPPLEMENT YOUR BIBLICAL STUDIES, PRAYER AND "STILL TIME" WITH GOD DURING THE FAST.

Before embarking on this particular fast, I NEVER, and I mean ever, listened to sermons online. For some reason, I felt opposed to online preachers, TBN, or any remote gospel teaching; quite honestly and erroneously, I believed it was for "lazy Christians" and "fake prosperity teaching preachers."

Most of the preachers I found, with the exception of a few friends recommendations, were new to me. With that being said, although I did basic research on all the preachers I listened to and ensured they were in line with core Biblical principles, please do not take the listing of the resources I employed as advertising and endorsing all the preacher's beliefs, but rather as an endorsement of the messages in the videos I have particularly recommended.

God can use anybody (Numbers 22:21-29), and God definitively used these preachers to drive home, make plain, and emphasize the messages and themes that I was seeking

God for. A few of these sermons were literally LIFE-CHANGING for me, but my heart was also so open for correction, repentance, and being more like Christ. God was faithful to let me find what I was seeking in accordance with His will.

The same goes for the music choices. I am sure some of these artists have some discoverable infractions in their walk with Christ; however, it was the Holy Spirit's anointing of the songs that resonated with me. I realize there are entire "ministries" dedicated to fault-finding in other professed Believers and making spectacles from their stumbles and falls; however, this guide does not ascribe to that lane. I will never ignore outright open rebellion to God's word in my selection of worship and study tools, but I will also never be on a speck-finding mission. (Matthew 7:5)

The work of growth and self-actualization in the Lord is a full and beautiful one. I have found that when truly doing that work, there is little time for researching ways to rebuke our brothers and sisters, particularly when the offenses are outside of relationship and connectivity. Basically, when you are really doing the work of the Lord in your own flesh, you have very little time to focus on the faults of others.

TIPS, EXAMPLES & EXPERIENCES

From a practical standpoint, the 8-12 hours I recommend is a lot of time, and if you have it, it should be executed wisely. In addition to the Holy Spirit and biblically inspired scriptures I extracted to read, study, and meditate on, I prayed multiple times during the day, and I watched sermons and discussions on the precepts and daily biblical principles I focused on during the fast. I used a combination of YouTube, the YouVersion Bible App, and friends' recommendations to search out these tools. I also selected worship music that coincided with the daily reading or that my soul hungered for.

The specific sermons and music artists will be listed in my sample guide, but again, I implore you to seek God and use the methods I suggested to research tools that are fitting for your journey on the Fast God chose for you.

(STEP 2) ACTION 8: ORGANIZE OR CONSTRUCT YOUR FASTING OUTLINE

I have included a template for you to organize the information gathered in **Actions 1– 7.** You may also use a free writing space of your choice; I used a spiral notebook the first time. I have also included my own outline for that first comprehensive biblical fast. I did leave subsections out for brevity so as not to limit or bias your own request. Make sure your outline reflects your true desires and requests for God. I will expound on my outline and the methodology in Part 2 of this guidance, "The Journey." All sermons and music listed can be searched on YouTube.

IMPORTANT NOTE:

Without negating the ministry that this book is accomplishing by passing along information that took me years through God's Word and Spirit to become aware of and discover, I still must say this:

There are invaluable gems to be discovered when we search God's word firsthand. One scripture may lead to another, and a word may jump out to you that didn't jump out to me that leads you to another scripture not on this list because we are different, our lives are different, and our challenges are different, albeit all running the same race. As urged throughout this guide, pray and petition God on how He wants you to go about this journey, and if something feels unaddressed or unanswered by this list or any information provided in this guide, it is your duty to seek the missing pieces out. "Study and do your best to present yourself to God approved, a workman [tested by trial] who has no reason to be ashamed, accurately handling and skillfully teaching the word of truth." (2 Timothy 2:15)

TIPS, EXAMPLES & EXPERIENCES

My First Biblical Fast: After reading Isaiah 58, studying, and praying through it, God led me to make it my overarching scripture for this fast and now this book. After I prayed every morning, it was the first scripture I read daily before the sun came up. (originally handwritten, now typed for ease of reading)

STEP 3
PHYSICAL PREPARATIONS

intentionally left the physical prep for this journey last, after all of the categorically spiritual. I did this to drive home the point that this is not for dieting or weight loss, and the goal is to be completely spiritually minded by the time you consider the physical aspect of this journey. I will frame the following as 'I did' statements as I am only outlining my personal experience vs. advising you on what to do, although I will give some DO NOTS.

*I DID

eat solely fruits and vegetables for 3 days prior to the time I would be embarking on the fast. This was about 1/4 of the time of my total fast of 14 days. I based this on my prior experiences of loading up before fasting and/or eating heavy foods prior to a water fast only to experience extreme fasting side effects like headaches, constipation, fatigue, cottonmouth, body aches, and fever.

*I DID

exercise before the fast but ceased exercising about 3 days into the fast to preserve my energy. This proved to be smart, as in the last three days of the fast, I experienced extreme fatigue and body weakness.

I DID

do a body check before starting. I checked my blood pressure and blood sugar to ensure a range of normality. I also assessed any body aches and pains and noted them.

I DID

alert my loved ones I would not be available by phone for the duration. I told my loved ones that I was going on a spiritual journey and would be available in an emergency, checking in by group text when led. I did not tell folks I was fasting; You do not fast for compliment seeking.

DO NOT

load up on food, liquor, or ungodly activity like it is some sort of bachelorette party before the wedding (which, sidenote, is also a very unproductive and counterintuitive practice for marriage).

You will pay for this physically and spiritually. Your body will hurt, your head will hurt, your blood sugars will go buck wild, and you will not be able to withstand the natural side effects of fasting.

PREPARATION SUMMARY

Remember, you are doing all of this preparation BEFORE YOU FAST; for me, this all took less than one week.

THE JOURNEY

Many times, we spend so much time researching, studying, and preparing for a task that we never actually embark on it. For this reason, I will not belabor the rest of this guidance; I want you to get to it. I do, however, want to take some time to expound on my personal experience during the fast outlined in the above guidance.

Again, I firmly state that **you should fast from and sustain yourself with whatever God leads you to**. In the Bible, I only found evidence of a water fast and a dry fast; however, in my case, God said STRICTLY WATER AND NATURAL TEA WITHOUT ADDITIVES for 13 days.

STICK TO IT! The actual fasting from food is just as serious as all other parts of the fast, and if you cannot deny yourself whatever God has commanded or you have committed to God to deny for the entire duration without wavering, your sacrifice is not a true sacrifice.

People have said to me, "I have to attend a birthday party on this day, or so and so invited me to lunch, or my birthday falls on the fast, or I got hungry; can I eat after 6 p.m.?" Again, I am militant here and will only pass on my experience, and the answer to all is NO, NO, NO. I don't even want to say don't schedule the fast during festive times because the point of a fast is sacrifice and obedience, not convenience.

Whatever leads you to fasting should be more important than all of the above. Birthdays, dinners, etc., will still be there, and you have experienced them all. You know how drinks feel, how a turn-up feels, how watching ungodly movies feels, and how partaking in unwholesome talk feels–all of which threaten the effectiveness of your fast. But do you know how your next level feels? Have you tasted how God makes all things new when you present your body as a living sacrifice, holy and pure unto Him?

BEWARE OF WARFARE

Remember, you are taking on a spiritually beneficial endeavor. Beneficial to the Kingdom of God. The fasting that God chooses has the express purpose and intention to "undo the bonds of wickedness, to tear to pieces the ropes of the yoke, to let the oppressed go free, and break apart every [enslaving] yoke" (Isaiah 58:6). **Where there are the oppressed, there is an oppressor. Where there is bondage, there is a captor.**

OUR ENEMY WILL NOT ROLL OVER AND PLAY DEAD;

IT WILL NOT LET YOU GO WITHOUT A FIGHT

AND WILL DO EVERYTHING, I MEAN ERRTHANG, TO DETER YOU, DISRUPT YOU, DISCOURAGE YOU, DECEIVE YOU, AND DISADVANTAGE YOU DURING THIS FAST!

In my case, the enemy stirred up the strongest warfare I had seen in years in the very areas where I was seeking breakthroughs. During this first biblical fast, my husband did not speak to me from about Day 4 to literally the last day, Day 13. During the fast, the Lord led me to speak up on an injustice in our home that I had been afraid of speaking about for years due to being apprehensive about the same type of emotional backlash it inevitably led to. But like Naman when told to dip in the Jordan seven times and like Joshua when God instructed him to march around Jericho seven times, I did not get discouraged by my husband's retaliation on Days 5, 6, 7, 10, or 13, for I knew it was responsive warfare to my act of obedience. I believed God would do what He said He would do, and on the very last day of the fast, the yoke broke!

Hallelujah! God did not forget me or forsake me, but it took for me to be steadfast, unmovable, and always abounding in the Word of God, the Will of God in this fast, and the commitments I professed to God at the outset of this fast. No, it was not easy when the hell showed up in full force on day 5 of the fast, when the hunger was getting real. Front row.

Of course, that serpent of old whispers–"water is just a zero calorie liquid, can't you just have a little soup broth?"

"Put a little honey in that tea; your sugar is surely low." "What you need is some holy wine!"

The enemy will also visit you in your time of sanctification during this fast with LIES:

"You are fasting for a marriage breakthrough, and she is getting worse. Just masturbate."

"Sermons all day?! Nah, God said you need rest, and pleasures are at His right hand; go ahead and watch a little [Scandal, Housewives, Play PS5, Go to Strip Club]. Pick your pleasure."

"Wine is a liquid too, and pickles have no calories; they won't break your fast."

"Your body is too weak to wake up at your set time. Sleep in. Hey, you took off work anyway."

"They are getting on your nerves; why pray to God? He will take His time answering; your non- believer, unmarried family member is just a call away. Hey, God speaks through people, right?"

"Just roll up, put on your favorite music, and "zen out." It'll be easier to 'meditate.' God speaks to you more clearly when you are high, anyway."

"Humility? Submission? It sounds like God just wants you to be a doormat!"

"If you eat something for just one day, you can always go back to your fast. God knows your heart" (yeah, He does), and it is deceitful in all its ways (Jeremiah 17:9).

"You need to forgive others, right? So go ahead and just call him or her up–just to say you forgive them, of course."

To all these possible lies, I give the same remedy:

GET BEHIND ME, SATAN!!!

(MATTHEW 4:10-11)

Coming into this fight with the right heart, mindset, and understanding is essential to reaping the full benefits of the fast, which is equivalent to success. Do not forget or underestimate this.

TIPS, EXAMPLES & EXPERIENCES

I will now give you a play-by-play example of one of my days during the fast. This fast was during summertime, when the kids were home from school, and I was working from home.

MY JOURNEY: WHAT A DAY LOOKED LIKE

5:45 A.M.

I set the alarm and woke up at 5:45 (I wanted to beat the sun daily), relieved myself (you pee a lot), and before brushing my teeth or eating, I headed to the living room to pray so as not to disturb Hubby or the kids. I opened up the curtain to the sliding doors that led to the balcony that overlooked the ocean to allow the near sunrise to flood into the room. I then grabbed one of my large sofa pillows and threw it to the floor, opened up my Bible, and started to read Isaiah 58.

I read and then stopped and prayed the scripture, read, and reread and prayed the scripture, and then transitioned into prayer. This usually ended in a face full of tears and me lying prostrate before God. I rose and went for the notebook that I used for the fast (I tried to abstain from as much technology as possible) and reviewed my focal point for the day. The mornings, more than anything, were my quiet time with God; it was the most selfless time for me to do this and not feel isolated from my family.

6:35 A.M.

I then grabbed my 1-liter bottle of water and started to read the scriptures that I gathered from my prep related to the topic. I studied until I heard the kids or husband moving around.

7:45/8:30 A.M.

At this point, I would get up and brush my teeth, then greet them with hugs and kisses. Then we would have family prayers and listen to worship songs. Sometimes it would be all of us, sometimes just myself and the kids.

8:45/9:15 A.M.

I would then prepare breakfast for the family, and while they ate, I would sit at the table with them and consume the delicious Word of God.

9:45- 12 NOON

The kids would start their summer studies (academic and biblical), and I would either continue with my reading of scripture if I had not finished it or go to YouTube on our TV to start my sermon or media studies for the day. I liked to use the TV as opposed to my laptop and headphones, when possible, to share information with my family and to isolate, even if it was just by earshot. Most times, I had not finished my scriptural studies and did not get to start multimedia studies until the early afternoon.

NOON

At noon, I would break and prepare lunch, and when lunch was served again, I would sit with the family with the Word and water. I did not ever feel left out or appear downtrodden, as I knew that would make my family feel bad for me not eating, and I was genuinely grateful for the spiritual meal before me. I usually excused myself from lunch early to go stretch, work out, and/or lie down for a period of 20 to 40 minutes, depending on how I felt that day as far as my physical energy. The kids would usually join me after working out or stretching, or they would come out just to play.

2:00 P.M.

I would go inside and start to prep for dinner and play worship music and/or put on a sermon, lecture, or biblical discussion in my headphones, but usually, music.

3:00/3:15 PM

Whilst the food was cooking, I would sit down for afternoon studies, which started with prayer, and then proceeded with media studies, usually via YouTube. I would take notes anytime I watched sermons or discussions, go over them, and try to find myself in the messages. I would look for relevant takeaways, applications, and future guidance. I would also review my notes before bed. I must admit, hearing multiple sermons every day as opposed to once a week was one of the highlights for me of fasting and a practice I extracted from the fast and later my family employed daily. We now listen to sermons and/or biblical talks online daily– sometimes several times a day. #JesusNerds

5/6 PM

We would have dinner between 5 and 6. At dinner, I would do the same thing, but this is where, as a family, we discussed our day, things we learned, and our children's attempts at the memory verses they are assigned weekly. We would laugh and talk at dinner, which helped me tremendously in those more challenging days.

7/7:30 PM

Here, we would usually watch a sermon together or a Christian movie, or our children would do some creative writing together while my husband and I spent quality time on the days when he did not isolate, as shared above.

8:30/9 PM

I would turn in fairly early during the fast; it was essential to me being invigorated for the days to come. I would pray over my focal points, for people in my life, and give God thanks for the many blessings, conditions, tests, and God's holiness and character. I would then put worship music in my headphones because Hubby would, at this time of our lives, usually be up watching television and going to sleep. I enjoyed peaceful rest most days of the fast, with some intense dreams on a few days, and did not end up needing the alarm as I naturally rose from 5:30-5:45 a.m. daily.

SOME TAKEAWAYS

Fasting is much less burdensome when your home environment is spirit-led and filled. Our family was at the beginning stages of developing a spiritual flow and routine when I performed this fast, but even this helped tremendously with the fasting because I did not feel alienated by it. We now have a much more involved and full family cooperative flow, which eases the spiritual burdens I experienced in that season of fasting. For example, I pray daily in the morning, as well as my husband and I together. We have devotions where we watch a sermon daily, we pray collectively two-three times daily as a family, and we watch sermons or Christian discussions in the afternoons. Therefore, fasting now is inevitably less of an isolated practice for me besides eating. I find my fast now being more comprised of solo prayer and study versus multimedia for this reason.

I experienced some physical side effects that I want to highlight:

- ➢ Sometimes, I woke up with a faster heartbeat, just at the beginning of the day when I rose.
- ➢ Less than desirable breath and the need to brush several times a day, albeit only consuming
- ➢ After about Day 3, I did not have any bowel movements until about Day 10, which was only once, and the consistency was that of a 3- month-old breastfed baby.

- ➤ Lightheadedness when moving from a sitting position to standing, causing a need to pause and be still for roughly 10 seconds before walking.
- ➤ Red eyes
- ➤ Again, especially if you do a fast beyond 7 days, you will lose an immense amount of weight. I limited my exercise to low-impact cardio, such as moderate walks, stretching, and swimming. The thinner you are, the more of a concern this will likely be. I had some wiggle room.

This first fast and every fast thereafter always put this world in its rightful place, reminding me that I am in it but not of it. I was already deactivated from all social media prior to this fast by spiritual unction, but the fast further solidified how social media, television, and entertainment, in general, have much too much influence, control, and consideration for us as believers and free humans. The stuff we allow to consume our time and thoughts is really so trivial. Every day I continued on the fast, and this started to become bolder and surer in my heart. If I could live without food, certainly these trivialities of hair, nails, makeup, clothes, shoes, name brands, drinks, sweets, social media, entertainment, anger, resentment, and depression WOULD NOT CONTROL ME. So, fasting, for me, really does put food in its rightful place, as well as some other seemingly necessary life offerings. Fasting allowed me to see how much time and thought I put into food. Fasting allowed me to identify how tightly connected food and social interaction were for me. Fasting is truly a chain breaker, as identified in Isaiah 58:6.

HERE ARE A FEW EXCERPTS FROM MY OVERALL JOURNEY:

- ➤ I DID drink spring water, sparkling mineral water, and tea without sugar or any other additives.
- ➤ When God tells me to water fast, it is not negotiable; it does not end at 6 p.m., and it does not have cheat days. I drank 32-64 ounces of water per day.

➤ No purified water ever. Water does not equal liquids; if God said water, it's water, and liquor, coconut water, water beverages, juice, and sweetened teas are not water.

AND YES, JESUS TURNED WATER INTO WINE, BUT, BABY, IT IS NOT WATER! KAPEESH!

➤ I DID NOT drink coffee, any type of juice, broth, chew gum, drink juice, take vitamins, or eat food of any kind for the entire duration of the fast.

➤ I DID get plenty of sleep. I did not really sleep during the day, but I did retire early. This was mainly to support my discipline from idle time, leisurely activities, and to combat the fatigue that naturally comes with water fasting.

➤ I DID NOT watch any movies, read any books, or listen to any music that was not created for the direct and explicit purpose of glorifying the living God.

➤ I DID have immense energy for the majority of the fast. I did swim, praise dance, and engaged in physical play with my children during the fast. Although I deviated from my normal exercise after the first three days, I was astounded by how energized I was compared to other water fasts.

➤ I DID abstain from sex for 3 days, and those days were selected by my husband and me during the fast. We did this in accordance with scripture and by agreement on a time period in the middle of the fast. There is nothing unholy about marital sex; this was a personal choice for me as a sacrifice because of my love and enjoyment of daily sex with my husband.

➤ I DID experience healing of a chronic upper abdominal pain I had. The pain dissipated six days into the fast and has not returned.

➤ I DID NOT participate in any arguments. My marriage was in a rough patch, which is one of the reasons why I was so no-nonsense with adhering to my commitments during the fast because I could not do it without God's close presence, clear guidance, and comfort. Despite my husband being in one of the worst demeanors of our marriage–the 13 days of the fast were strife-free, argument-free, and contention-free, to the glory of God!

➢ I DID have to cook for my family for the majority of the days I was fasting. Every time I felt tempted to give into my flesh's desires–not needs–I instantly went into prayer, but the gravity of the things I was asking for and the anticipation of actually receiving them always greatly outweighed these temptations. For some reason, I get so creative with my cooking when I fast.

➢ I DID lose 23 pounds during this. I put this last, and I put this only to advise those who may be on the thinner side of how much weight this length of a water fast can take off of them.

EXCERPTS FROM THIS 13-DAY FAST'S BENEFITS:

➢ Newness and Revival

➢ Spiritual Direction

➢ Six new ministries birth

➢ Two new businesses birth

➢ Mental Clarity

➢ Physical Wellness

➢ Life reconstruction

➢ Increased closeness to God

➢ More clearly defined my purpose

This Book

UNPACKING FROM THE JOURNEY
DAY 1 TO THE REST OF YOUR LIFE

A fter I finished the 13-day biblical water fast, I had roughly 76 pages of notes and journaling, a renewed spirit, a reset vision, and a vigor to reclaim and repair.

Again, the fast is not magic; you have to use the virtue power gained from this experience to see every revelation come to fruition. What God spoke during the fast applies henceforth and forever more.

Keep your notes close, review them often, and when led to go deeper than before, gear up again for the increase.

MY 13 DAY
CUSTOMIZABLE
FAST

DAY 1
ALL MY REQUEST & INTENTIONS PRIOR TO STUDY

1. GETTING MY HOUSE IN ORDER/SELF AND FAMILY

a) Husband Taking Kingdom Position

b) Stability and Consistency of Spirituality in Family (Marriage and Kids)

c) My own Spiritual Growth & Total Reliance & Trust in God in matters of my Family

d) Spiritual Health of Our Children.

  ➢ Discovering their spiritual gifts and propensities.

  ➢ Asking God to increase their love of the Bible and spiritual growth activities.

e) Strategy for Spiritual Warfare

FOCUS SCRIPTURES:

Isaiah 58, Exodus 34, Exodus 39

HOLY SPIRIT LED FOCUSES

> ➤ Spiritual Growth

TOOLS

SERMONS (YOUTUBE):

> ➤ Tony Evans - Portrait of a Christian Family
>
> ➤ How Do I Love God More Than My Entertainment? // Ask Pastor John Tony Evans- The Strategy of Satan What Is Idolatry? // Ask Pastor John Tony Evans- Kingdom Man Full Idol Worship Today: 6 Modern Idols We Still Worship Rafer Owens- Can't Stop, Won't Stop Kingdom Men Rising Film Preview.

DAY 2
WRITING THE VISION & PREPARING TO RECEIVE GOD'S LAW FOR MY LIFE

⎯⎯⎯⎯ ༄ ⎯⎯⎯⎯

1. Journaling

2. Revelations

3. Things l need to do and want to do for God

4. God's promises to me

FOCUS SCRIPTURES:

Isaiah 58, Genesis 15, Genesis 46:1-5, Numbers 12, Deuteronomy 13:1-5,1 Kings 3, 1 Samuel 3, Habakkuk 2, 1 John 1:9, Psalm 85, Psalm 67, Psalm 23, Hebrew 13, John 14, 2 Thessalonians 3 1 John 2, James 2, Galatians 3, 2 Peter 1, 2 Peter 3, Hebrews 6, Psalm 105, Psalm 119:140-65, Josiah 23, Isaiah 38, Acts 13, Romans 4, Hebrews 4, Isaiah 41:10, Isaiah 26:3, Deuteronomy 31:8, Psalm 37:23-24, 2 Corinthians 12:9-10, Isaiah 40:31, Jeremiah 29:11, and Philippians 4:6-9, James 1:2-7, Exodus 14:14, Romans 8:28, Isaiah 43:2, Isaiah 54:10-18, 1 John 1:9, John 3:16 John 3:36, John 8:30-40, Psalm 34:17,

Romans 10:9-11, Proverbs 3:4-7, James 5:14 -17, Matthew 6:31-33, Matthew 7:9-11, Luke 11:9-13, Romans 8:31-35, Ephesians 3:16-19, John 14:13-16, Psalm 103:2-5

HOLY SPIRIT LED FOCUSES

➤ Vision for My Family

TOOLS

SERMONS:

➤ Tony Evans- Raising Kingdom Kids Loving Your Woman

➤ Respecting Your Man

➤ A Challenge to Higher Standards

➤ Tony Evans- Becoming a Kingdom Wife pt 1-3

➤ Overcoming In Christ | Sermon by Tony Evans

➤ Your Time Is Now - Tony Evans Sermon

DAY 3
OBEDIENCE

———— ৯৫৬ ————

1. Promise of Peace
2. Promise of Productivity
3. Promise of God's Presence

FOCUS SCRIPTURES:

Isaiah 58, Leviticus 26, 1 Samuel 12:14-16, 2 Samuel 12:9-14, 1 Kings 9:3-9, 2 Kings 22:18-20, Daniel 1:8-9, 1 Corinthians 7:19, Exodus 19:4-8, Deuteronomy 4, Exodus 34:10-11, Deuteronomy 11, 27, 28, 32, Exodus 20, Proverbs 6:20-26, Exodus 19, Joshua 1:7-9, 2 Kings 17:7-20, 1 Samuel 15, Psalm 40:6-8,Proverbs 21:1-5 Jeremiah 7:19-34, Hebrews 12, James 4:7-8, 1 John 5:1-5, John 14:12-15, Galatians 6:1-8, Hebrews 5:7-14, Romans 13, 1 Peter 2:13-20, Hebrews 13:7, 17-19 Ephesians 6:1-9, Colossians 3:1-25, Acts 4:16-22, Acts 5:27-32, Titus 1:15

HOLY SPIRIT LED FOCUSES

➢ Obedience

TOOLS
MUSIC:

➢ Fred Hammond & RFC - Let the Praise Begin Tye Tribbett - Work It Out

➢ Praise Him In Advance - Marvin Sapp

➤ Your Still Holy| Elevation Worship & Maverick

➤ City, Still Holy (fat. Ryan Oféi & Naomi Raine) | TRIBL Let The Praise Begin - YouTube

SERMONS

➤ Tony Evans Sermon Idolatry of Religion Tony Evans Sermon- Idol Culture

➤ Tony Evans- Loving the Wrong World Tony Evans- Idol - Pleasure

➤ What Do My Entertainment Habits Reveal About My Soul? // Ask Pastor John

➤ How Much Entertainment Is Too Much? // Ask Pastor John

➤ Stop Blocking Your Miracle- Tony Evans

➤ A Challenge to Obedience - Tony Evans Sermon

➤ Dr. Tony Evans | Obedience: The Response of Spiritual Growth

➤ A Tale of Two Men | Sermon by Tony Evans The Value of Obedience- Tony Evans

➤ Priscilla Shirer: YOUR Spiritual Battle & the Armor of God (Full Teaching)

DAY 4
CONFESSION OF SINS, SHOW SORROW FOR SINS

—————— ⁓๑෧⁓ ——————

1. The result of confessing sin

2. First step in true repentance.

FOCUS SCRIPTURES:

Isaiah 58, Psalm 51, 1 King 21, Jonah 3, Nehemiah 9, Numbers 14, Numbers 12: 9-15, 2 Samuel 12:13, Psalm 32:1-6, Nehemiah 1:4-11, Isaiah 6:4-9, Luke 5:1-11, Luke 18:11-14, Leviticus 5:1-6, Matthew 6:5-15, Psalm 38:17- 22, Isaiah 59, Jeremiah 14:7-12, Daniel 9:3-23, Proverbs 28:13-14, 1 John 1:5-10, James 5:16-20, Matthew 10:32 - 33, Romans 10:9-10

HOLY SPIRIT LED FOCUSES

➢ Confession of Sins

TOOLS

SERMONS:

➢ Dr. Tony Evans | Sin: The Hindrance of Spiritual Growth Dr. Tony Evans | Scripture: The Food of Spiritual Growth

> ➤ Why Do We Confess If Our Sins Are Already Forgiven? // Ask Pastor John

> ➤ The Believer's Confession of Sin (Psalm 51) Grace to You

MUSIC:

> ➤ Wait On You | Elevation Worship & Maverick City New York Restoration Choir - Speak To My Heart Fred Hammond & RFC - Let the Praise Begin

DAY 5
REPENTANCE
BEING SORRY FOR SIN AND TURNING TO GOD

Genuine repentance is a prerequisite for God's In response to repentance, God would bring restoration and blessing.

JOEL 2, JONAH 3

Command to repent - *Zechariah 1:3– 6, Jeremiah 18:9–12, Ezekiel 18, Acts 17, 2 Peter 3, Mark 1, Luke 13, Revelation 2, Revelation 3, Matthew 3, Mark 6, Acts 2, Acts 3, Acts 26, Luke 24*

ASPECTS OF REPENTANCE

a) Acknowledging we are lost (Luke 15)

b) Expressing sorrow for sin (Luke 5)

c) Returning to the Father (Luke 15)

d) Believing in Jesus Christ (Mark 1; Revelation 3; Acts 20)

e) Ceasing ungodly works and doing good works (Acts 3:8)

THE RESULTS OF REPENTANCE

a) Escape from disaster (Jeremiah 18)

b) Forgiveness (1 King 8; Acts 2:8-47)

c) Salvation (2 Corinthians 7:8-2)

d) A new heart & spirit (Ezekiel 18:19 - 31)

e) A knowledge of the truth (2 Timothy 2:14 - 26)

f) Eternal life (Acts 11:16 -18)

g) Regret without repentance brings death (Matthew 27:1– 5, 2 Corinthians 7:9–11)

All verses relating to repentance instruct you to confess your sins, change your thinking, turn away from sin, seek God for direction in your life, and show fruit/produce fruit consistent with repentance, which is essentially demonstrating new behavior that proves a change of heart and a conscious decision to turn away from sin.

HOLY SPIRIT LED FOCUSES

➢ Repentance

TOOLS

MUSIC:

➢ Bow Down - Bishop Paul Morton and Full Gospel Fellowship How excellent by Mississippi Mass Choir

SERMONS:

➢ Going Beyond Ministries with Priscilla Shirer - Fervent in Prayer, The Key to Your Reversal - Tony Evans Sermon

DAY 6
HUMILITY
LOWLINESS AND FREEDOM FROM PRIDE

"...Holy, Holy, Holy..." To say the word "Holy" twice in Hebrew is to describe someone as most. To say the word three times intensifies the idea to its highest level. Our greatest failing is not only realizing who God is but also what His character is like. This is particularly true in the case of God's holiness.

ISAIAH 6:3

To be holy means "to be set apart." God is set apart from the power, practice, and presence of sin and is set apart to ABSOLUTE RIGHTEOUSNESS & GOODNESS. There is no sin in God, and God can have nothing to do with sin. If we are to approach God, we must do so on God's terms. We must be made holy by God's action in Christ.

Most of our lives are so caught up in the mundane that we don't understand and experience God's holiness as we should. There is little appreciation or understanding of the sacred "otherness" of God. We have too often reduced Him to only a friend and advisor. We do so at our own peril, for it is that sacred "otherness" that brings us to our knees. That is where the relationship needs to begin. Isaiah received God's call to that position. He recognized

God's holiness and His own uncleanness and the need for God to purify Him before He would be fit to serve as a prophet. The experience of coming to understand God's holiness is simultaneously humble, challenging, and exhilarating. We touch the fullness of our potential as we are touched and purified by God in Christ's sacrifice for us.

HUMILITY INVOLVES:

a) A childlike attitude, not children, are teachable, blindly obedient to their divine authority, loving, easy to forgive, in good spirits for the most part, in discriminatory and don't hold grudges (Matthew 18:1-4).

b) Repentance (Isaiah 66:2, Luke 18:13-14).

c) Submission before God (2 Chronicles 34:27).

d) Seeking God's Face in Prayer and Fasting (2 Chronicles 7:10-15, Ezra 8:21, Psalm 35:13).

e) Following God's Law (Jeremiah 44:10, Zephaniah 2:3).

f) Working for Justice and Mercy (Micah 6:6-8).

g) Opposite of Pride (Proverbs 3:34, Daniel 4:37, 1 Peter 5:5).

BENEFITS OF HUMILITY:

a) God saves the humble (1 Corinthians 1:26- 29)

b) God gives the humble grace (James 4:6).

c) God raises the lowly (Job 5:11).

d) God revives the lowly (Isaiah 57:15).

e) God honors the humble (Proverbs 18:12).

f) God rewards the humble (Proverbs 22:4).

g) With humility comes wisdom (Proverbs 11:2).

h) Jesus is the perfect example of Humility: John 3:16-27, John 13:4-5

FOCUS SCRIPTURES:

Isaiah 58, Psalm 35

HOLY SPIRIT LED FOCUSES:

➤ Humility and Obedience

TOOLS:

SERMONS/SPOKEN WORD

➤ Be Humble or You'll Stumble - Philippians 2:8-11 Skip Heitzig

➤ The Sin of Elitism | Sermon by Tony Evans

➤ Going Beyond Ministries with Priscilla Shirer-Acting in Obedience

➤ I Have a New Name (Spoken Word) - Hosanna Wong

SONGS:

➤ Daryl Coley - II Chronicles

DAY 7
FASTING FOR NATIONAL NEED
GOD HELP US!

1. Revelation of truth in the world

2. Promulgation of revealed truth

3. Rise of Kingdom citizens

4. My role

5. Study of the Prophets

FOCUS SCRIPTURES:

Isaiah 58, 2 Chronicles 2, Ezra 8, The Book of Esther

HOLY SPIRIT LED FOCUS

➢ Government

TOOLS

SERMONS:

➢ Tony Evans Kingdom Politics series (5 videos)-

➢ The Prophets: A Quick Overview | Whiteboard Bible Study

MUSIC:

➢ Jireh | Elevation Worship & Maverick City

➢ Daryl Coley - II Chronicles

DAY 8
DEEPEN MY PRAYER LIFE/ DAY OF PRAYER & PRAISE
DIRECT COMMUNICATION WITH GOD

———— ✎✎✎ ————

What is prayer- Calling on the name of the Lord, calling to God, seeking God's face, approaching God's throne of grace, drawing near to God.

1. Thanksgiving

2. Confession

3. Intercession

4. Pray 8 Work - Nehemiah 4

FOCUS SCRIPTURES:

Isaiah 58, Daniel 9, Nehemiah 1, Nehemiah 2, 2 Corinthians 12:8-9, 1 Thessalonians 5:16-21, Psalm 27:8-10, Psalm 34:4, Isaiah 55, Psalm 25:1-2, Psalm 86:4-13, Psalm 141:1-2, Psalm 28:1-2, Philippians 4:6-9, John 17:6-20, Psalm 27:4-10, John 14:12, Psalm 145:18, Proverbs 1:7-2:25, Mark 11:24, Psalm 34:4, James 1:5, 2 Chronicles 6:37, Luke 11:9-13, Luke 18:1-8, James 4:1-10, Matthew 6:5-15

HOLY SPIRIT LED FOCUSES

➤ Prayer/Hindrances to Prayer

TOOLS

SERMONS:

➤ How Do I Know If I'm Doing Enough for God? // Ask Pastor John

➤ Am I Completely Surrendered to Christ? // Ask Pastor John

➤ The Secret to Powerful Prayer - Tony Evans Sermon

MUSIC:

➤ DARYL COLEY - II CHRONICLES

➤ Joy Unspeakable - Dallas/Fort Worth Mass Choir Donnie McClurkin Great is Your Mercy

DAY 9
TODAY I WILL FACE A GIANT IN MY LIFE

————————— ༄༅༄ —————————

FOCUS SCRIPTURES:

Isaiah 58, 2 Samuel 12, Joshua 1:1-9, Psalm 18:29-50, Philippians 4:11-13, Exodus 5:1-4, Exodus 10:24-29, Judges 7:1-24, 1 Samuel 17:26-50, Esther 5:1-8, Daniel 3:1-30, Daniel 6:1-23, Acts 4:1-5:41, Deuteronomy 31:6,1 Corinthians 16, Hebrew 3, Mark 6:50, Genesis 26, Philippians 4, Acts 4, Colossians 1, Romans 8:37-39, 2 Corinthians 5:137, Psalm 18:29-50, Psalm 46, 1 Corinthians 16

HOLY SPIRIT LED FOCUSES

➢ Prayer

DAY 10
TO LEARN THE WILL OF GOD IN MY LIFE

—————— ❧❧❧ ——————

God's will includes His Word, His Law and His Desires (Matthew 18:14)

Abah- to will, be willing, consent (Genesis 24:5)

Thelema- signifies a) objectively that which is willed, of the will of God, the gracious design

Bulema- a deliberate design, that which is purposed - Romans 9:19, 1 Peter 4:3. Knowing God's will but not doing it invokes strong condemnation. Romans 2:18

SEEKING GOD FOR:

1. Insight - Insight into His purposes and understanding of the spiritual. We must know, understand, and choose His will

2. Wisdom

3. Understanding-Psalm 40:8

FOOTNOTE OF PSALM 40:8

Knowing the will of God is not simply a vehicle for finding the right vocation for life's work. While vocation is important, it is only a small part of God's will. The will of God must be thought of in more comprehensive terms. The will of God is for everyone to live in such a way as to bring honor and glory to God. For different people, God may have very different things in mind.

We must continually stay in God's Word so that He can make clear to us what His will is for us. We must also be still, listen, and know that He is God.

The first step towards understanding God's will is believing in Christ (John 3:14-16). If we do not accept this gift from God, we will not be saved from judgment (Matthew 7:21). Second, scripture teaches us that it is God's will for every believer to be sanctified (2 Thessalonians 2:13- 17).

Third, the Bible declares God's will as it must be applied to our lives (Deuteronomy 29:29). This fact involves commands to be obeyed, principles to be followed, prohibitions of things to be avoided, and living examples to be imitated or shunned. God takes great joy in those who cheerfully do His will. Although the Bible is a comprehensive revelation of God's will, there are always decisions that we make that Scripture does not directly address. In order to know God's will in these situations, we need to be in fellowship with the Lord (1 John 1:6-7), seek principles from the Word (1 Corinthians 10:6), obtain advice from godly counselors (Proverbs 11:14), use common sense, and remember that God works through our own minds and He desires for us to do His will (Philippians 2:13).

FOCUS SCRIPTURES:

Isaiah 58, Daniel 9, Philippians 1:6, Psalm 27, 1 John 2:15-17, 2 Timothy 3:16, Psalm 25, 1 Peter 4:1-2, 1 Peter 2:15, 1 Thessalonians 4:3, 1 Thessalonians 5:14, John 4:34, John 6:40, Hebrew 10:5-7, Romans 8:28, Acts 18:21

HOLY SPIRIT LED FOCUSES

> ➢ God's Will

TOOLS

SERMONS

- ➢ Going Beyond Ministries with Priscilla Shirer - Passion Conference 2018

- ➢ How Do I Find God's Will for My Life? // Ask Pastor John

- ➢ How to Know the Will of God Greg Laurie

DAY 11
MINISTRY/SPECIFIC CALLS

———— ୬୧୧ ————

FOCUS SCRIPTURES:

Isaiah 58, Acts 13:1-4, Acts 18:18-22, Philippians 3, Hebrews 3:1, Romans 11:27-30, Romans 8:28-31, 2 Thessalonians 2:13-14, Matthew 22:13-15, Ephesians 4:1, 1 Thessalonians 1:1-6, 2 Timothy 1:8-10, 1 Peter 2:20-21, 1 Corinthians 7:23-16, Colossians 3:14-16, Galatians 5:12-14, Romans 1:1-3, Acts 13:1- 3, Galatians 1:13-16, Romans 10:12-15

HOLY SPIRIT LED FOCUSES

➤ God's Will

TOOLS

SERMONS:

➤ I May Be Called to Missions – Where Do l Start?

➤ Ask Pastor John How Do I Know What My Spiritual Gift ls?

➤ *Activities* spiritualgiftstest.com

DAY 12
DECISION MAKING

————— ✤ —————

FOCUS SCRIPTURES:

Isaiah 58, 1 Corinthians 12:10, Hebrews 5:14, 1 Corinthians 14:1, 1 Corinthians 2:13, Luke 8

HOLY SPIRIT LED FOCUSES

➢ God's Will

TOOLS

SERMONS/GUIDANCES

➢ Ten tests for biblical decision making- Wretched YouTube Channel

➢ 2 Levels of Discernment (and signs of each)- Helen Calder

➢ Unlocking Spiritual Discernment - What If You Could See In The Spirit Realm- Grace for Purpose

➢ 5 Steps to Decision Making - How to Make the Right Decision Biblically | Jeremiah 41:17 Bible Munch

➢ Making Wise Decisions - Dr. Charles Stanley

➢ Do I Need to 'Hear from God' Before I Make a Decision? // Ask Pastor John

➢ "The Anointing On Your Life" | Luke 4:16-18- Rafer Owens

DAY 13
LIFT UP REQUEST OF DAY 1: REQUEST & INTENTIONS

1. GETTING MY HOUSE IN ORDER/SELF AND FAMILY

   a) Husband Taking Kingdom Position

   b) Stability and Consistency of Spirituality in Family (Marriage and Kids)

   c) My own Spiritual Growth & Total Reliance & Trust in God in matters of my Family

   d) Spiritual Health of Our Children.

2. STRATEGY FOR SPIRITUAL WARFARE

FOCUS SCRIPTURES:

Isaiah 58, Exodus 34, Exodus 39

HOLY SPIRIT LED FOCUSES:

➢ Spiritual Growth

TOOLS

SERMONS:

➢ The Motivation of Kingdom Stewardship - Tony Evans Sermon

➢ The Responsibility of Kingdom Stewardship - Tony Evans Sermon

➢ The Meaning of Stewardship - Tony Evans Sermon

➢ Do Not Worry • March 29 (Sermon Only, Tony Evans)

➢ Treasure in Your Trials • April 5 (Sermon Only, Tony Evans)

➢ Get Up & Go! Matthew 9:1-8- Rafer Owens

MUSIC:

➢ Shall Not Want | Elevation Worship & Maverick City

➢ Wait On You | Elevation Worship & Maverick City

➢ How excellent by Mississippi Mass Choir For

➢ You are great You do miracles so great by Min. Nene Iko

www.ingramcontent.com/pod-product-compliance
Lightning Source LLC
Chambersburg PA
CBHW041120120626
46547CB00019B/2791